All prices quoted in this book are obtained from a variety of auctions in various countries during the twelve months prior to publication and are converted to dollars at the rate of exchange prevalent at the time of sale.

DRAWINGS BY

PETER KNOX
PETER TENCH
DENISE FREEMAN

THE
LYLE
OFFICIAL
ANTIQUES
REVIEW 1983

THE
LYLE
OFFICIAL
ANTIQUES
REVIEW 1983

COMPILED BY MARGOT RUTHERFORD
EDITED by ANTHONY CURTIS

The publishers wish to express their sincere thanks
to the following for their kind help and assistance
in the production of this volume:

JANICE MONCRIEFF
NICOLA PARK
KAREN KILGOUR
JENNIFER KNOX
MAY MUTCH
CHRISTINE O'BRIEN
JOSEPHINE McLAREN
TANYA FAIRBAIRN
MARION McKILLOP
ELAINE HARLAND

The Library of Congress Cataloged This Serial as Follows:

The Lyle official antiques review.

Galashiels, Scot.ₗ
v.   Illus.   23 cm.   annual.
Began with 1971/72 issue. Cf. new serial titles.

1. Art objects—Collectors and collecting—Catalogs.
NK1133.L9   745.1   74-640592
MARC-S

ISBN 0-698-11190-7 hardcover
ISBN 0-698-11204-0 flexible binding
Printed in the United States of America
Distributed in the United States by Coward, McCann & Geoghegan,
200 Madison Avenue, New York, N.Y. 10016